Getting to Know Your Faith

Paul Steeves

InterVarsity Press
Downers Grove
Illinois 60515

InterVarsity Press is the book publishing
division of Inter-Varsity Christian Fellowship,
a student movement active on campus
at hundreds of universities, colleges and
schools of nursing. For information about local
and regional activities, write
IVCF, 233 Langdon St., Madison, WI 53703.

ISBN 0-87784-629-4
Library of Congress Catalog
Card Number: 76-55555

Printed in the
United States of America

STUDY OUTLINE

TOPIC E/JESUS' RETURN   103

Introduction

If theology can be shewn to be irrelevant to a living and evangelical faith, then the Church can afford to treat it with some indifference, and to leave its pursuit, like philosophy, to the Universities. But the Christian religion is theological or nothing. (P. T. Forsyth, The Person and Place of Jesus Christ, *Grand Rapids: Eerdmans, n.d., p. 3)*

Do You Want to Study Doctrine?/   The question itself sends shivers through many Christians. But at the same time they suspect that Forsyth may be right. Ideas do make a difference. And that is what doctrine really is: ideas about God and his contacts with us.

Every Christian must be interested in doctrine because every Christian thinks ideas about God and his truth. Doctrine need not be dull and dry as dust, although it often is. If we realize that doctrinal study helps us to think clearly about what is most important for the Christian believer, and if we cross the bridge from doctrine to our experience, Christian theology will come to life for us. At the same time the study of doctrine is no picnic. It requires effort. But if you will follow me, I hope that I can show you that, with a little work, the study of theology can be exciting.

The Scope of This Study/   In this study we will not investigate all of Christian teaching. Our outline has been provided by the five articles of the "Basis of Faith" of the Inter-Varsity Christian Fellowship of the United States. These articles affirm:

1. The unique divine inspiration, entire trustworthiness and authority of the Bible.
2. The deity of our Lord Jesus Christ.
3. The necessity and efficacy of the substitutionary death

of Jesus Christ for the redemption of the world, and the historic fact of his bodily resurrection.

4. The presence and power of the Holy Spirit in the work of regeneration.

5. The expectation of the personal return of our Lord Jesus Christ.

Some important distinctives of traditional Christianity are given little attention in this book. Naming just a few of these, we note that the concept of the Trinity, the doctrines of the church and church ordinances (for example, baptism), and the virgin birth of Jesus appear here only incidentally. The recent history of Christian thought explains this apparent distortion. During the past two centuries, the topics in this guide emerged as the distinguishing views of a current within Christianity usually designated as "evangelicalism." God, in his providence, has led the Inter-Varsity movement to be identified with this current from the movement's earliest stirrings at Cambridge University over one hundred years ago. As a result, the "Basis of Faith" which the Inter-Varsity Christian Fellowship of the United States adopted quite naturally reflected the distinctives of evangelicalism. Our study, then, focuses on the ideas which represent a particular emphasis within the whole body of Christian thinking. But because it covers doctrines which are foundational to the faith of all Christians, it is not exclusive but of interest and use to many.

More particularly, this guide can benefit officers who have been entrusted with the leadership of IVCF chapters. It is hoped that they will develop a greater appreciation for the ideas which God has called this movement to represent. Through this they may come to realize the historical significance of IVCF and of their participation in it. Similarly, this guide may aid others to understand Inter-Varsity's activity and, more importantly, to better understand the foundational truths of the Christian faith.

However, it should be clearly understood that this book

is not, in any way, an authoritative or definitive interpretation of the "Basis of Faith" adopted by the IVCF of the United States. It is only the approach of one person who has received immense benefit from the work of God through IVCF. I hope that this approach to these articles of faith will stimulate thoughtful students of God's Word to increase their own comprehension of Christian truth.

Material/ In addition to this study guide you will need (1) a Bible, preferably in modern-speech translation (the studies were prepared using the Revised Standard Version), and (2) a pen—recording discoveries as they are made in Bible study helps to shape and fix them in the mind. Spaces are provided in the guide for writing your answers. This extra step may seem to increase the study time, but it will prove its worth in the long run.

For Personal Study/ This study guide may be used for regular personal Bible study or in conjunction with a group's study of biblical doctrine. An individual can complete each study in about thirty minutes. The aim of this study guide is to help you interpret the passage for yourself. To accomplish this aim, first read the suggested passage and try to discover its most important features. Then answer the questions posed by the guide. Third, read the comments. The comments are not intended to be an exposition of the study passage. Rather, they are designed to stimulate further comprehension. For this reason, you should consider them only a minor part of the study.

Finally, think through the application questions; this is the step of making the passage relevant to your life. Application of biblical truth includes two elements: personal response to God himself as he reveals himself in Scripture, and translation of biblical truth into thinking and acting in daily life. Thus the application questions have been formulated to motivate you to think about your attitudes and relationship to God as well as about what he wants you to do.

With each study, some suggestions are made for further investigation. If time permits and interest motivates you, follow these suggestions. I encourage people using this guide to become acquainted with the durable doctrinal handbook by T. C. Hammond, *In Understanding Be Men* (IVP, 1968), which, since its first edition, has guided students of biblical doctrine for over forty years. Reference to this work is made at appropriate points. For those interested in traveling further into the regions of doctrinal study than this guide takes them, I suggest Gordon Lewis's *Decide for Yourself* (IVP, 1970).

For Group Study/ This guide, like its predecessors *Getting to Know Jesus* and *Getting to Know God,* was originally designed to be used by groups within a five-week period. The group studies one topic each week for five successive weeks. Following the suggestions given above for personal study, the individual participants prepare for the weekly group discussion by doing on their own the separate studies within the topics.

This pattern can be applied in several ways. For IVCF chapters and other large groups, a twenty-minute lecture followed by discussion in several small groups is probably the most profitable form of organization. The lecture should provoke thought about the topic as a stimulant to discussion. The discussion groups may concentrate on one of the studies or may take up questions raised by participants.

Experience has shown, however, that there are other ways to use this guide which are more appropriate to particular groups. For example, a group may dispense with the daily/weekly format which underlies the guide and use one study for each weekly discussion. Used in this way, this guide provides topics for up to thirty group sessions.

THE BIBLE

"The unique
divine inspiration,
entire trustworthiness
and authority
of the Bible."

God has spoken to people. He has revealed himself and the truth he wants us to know in written form. Throughout history, God's people have rejoiced in the belief that God gave them clear and authoritative information about himself, and how he wants them to believe and act.

How can we know that God has spoken uniquely in and through the Bible? We shall approach the doctrine of Scripture in our first topic by beginning with the claims which the Bible makes about itself. Of course, from a logical point of view, knowing that the Bible asserts that it comes from God and is the Word of God should not lead us, immediately, to accept the assertion as true. That would only be circular reasoning.

But it would not do for us to claim anything for the Bible that it does not claim for itself. If the Bible did not indicate that it is divinely inspired and should be accepted as authoritative, the evangelical view of Scripture would be hollow. But if the Bible does make these claims, then, as we shall see, the only consistent Christian view is one similar to that expressed in the article quoted above.

Thus, we shall endeavor to understand what the Bible says about the biblical writers and their words. Then we shall ask, Is that claim to be believed as true? To answer this question we shall consider Jesus' attitude toward Scripture, using the accounts of his life and teachings merely as reliable historical records, not as sacred Scriptures. The last two studies will explore the meaning of the Bible's authority.

study 1
peter's testimony to scripture

2 Peter 1:10-21

Questions

1/Peter has just written about the Christian conduct of his readers. What does he think he must do for them? Why?

_____

_____

_____

_____

2/To what two kinds of evidence does Peter point to show his readers that they were following the truth? (Cf. Mt. 17:1-8)

_____

_____

3/According to Peter, what is the relationship between his eyewitness account and written prophecy in confirming truth?

_____

_____

_____

4/How did Scripture come to be?

_____

_____

_____

5/Read 1 Peter 1:10-12. How does Peter describe the source of the prophets' writing (i.e., the Old Testament)? What similar thing does he say about the source of the apostles' message (that which became the New Testament)?

_____

_____

_____

6/According to 2 Peter 1:12-15, what function does Scripture serve for its readers? What is implied in verse 19 by the comparison with a light?

_____

_____

_____

Comments

Keenly aware that he will not always be with his readers, Peter points to the way in which they can remain convinced and alive in their Christian faith and conduct. To assure them that the story of Jesus is true he reminds them that he saw with his own eyes and heard with his own ears. He was there. God had confirmed Jesus' claim to be the Son of God.

But, Peter says, there is another source from which conviction comes: the prophetic word of Scripture. "Prophetic word" refers to all the writings of the people called "prophets," which we now call the Old Testament. A prophet was not merely a predictor of future events (although he often was that), but a person who proclaimed God's Word to society (see Deut. 18:17-22). The meaning of prophet is "one who speaks the words of another person" (see Ex. 7:1).

Scripture is a trustworthy source of truth because it comes from God. Scripture did not come merely through people trying to figure out truth for themselves. God "moved" the prophets. This verb is the word used to describe picking up a thing and carrying it to a goal (see, for example, Jn. 2:8; Mt. 14:11). It is used of the action of the wind (Acts 2:2; 27:15, 17). Peter maintains, then, that the message written in Scripture was the message God wanted written and caused to be written.

Application

1/Why should you pay attention to the Bible? How much attention should you give to the Bible?

2/How does Scripture function as a light for you? What kinds of darkness (psychological, intellectual, moral) do you find around you for it to dispell?

Further Study

1/Find a dictionary meaning of "scripture." What is the literal significance of the word? What is implied in its use to refer to the Bible? Read 2 Peter 3:15-16. What is implied by Peter's use of "other scriptures" in connection with a reference to Paul?

2/You can see more of Peter's and the disciples' view of the Old Testament in Acts. See especially, in their contexts, Acts 2:16-36; 3:18; 4:25; 10:43; 15:15-21. For what purposes did they use Scripture?

3/See *Thy Word Is Truth* by Edward J. Young (Grand Rapids: Eerdmans, 1957), especially pages 23-26.

4/Read verse 19 in several translations including the King James Version. You will find some discrepancy among translations which affects the way you answer question 3 (p. 12). The Revised Standard Version may suggest that the event of the transfiguration confirmed the Scripture as from God. There is good reason to conclude, however, that the KJV translation is preferable. On such a conclusion, Peter can be understood to assert that written Scripture is more solid assurance of truth than is an accurate account of a human experience. What are the implications of these divergent views?

study 2
paul's testimony to scripture

2 Timothy 3:10—4:5

Questions

1/To what experiences does Paul call Timothy's attention? What kinds of experience does he particularly emphasize?

_____

_____

2/What does Paul foresee? What is to be Timothy's response to such an event?

_____

_____

3/Why is Timothy to remain committed to the Scripture even though others defect from the truth?

_____

_____

4/What quality of the Scriptures insures that they will "instruct you for salvation" and equip the man of God for every good work?

5/How would you define "divine inspiration"?

6/In your own words, summarize what Paul says about Scripture.

Comments

The context in which Paul gives his testimony to Scripture is significant. He knows that there have always been persons who contradict the true doctrines of God, and he knows that they can be expected to be found in even more evil form in the future (note 3:1-9). And so Paul says that when Timothy sees the increase of human errors he must cling to that which is of divine origin—the teaching he received from Paul and the Scriptures of the Old Testament.

The crucial word of Paul's testimony to Scripture is *inspired.* Because we commonly speak of many acts and works of art, for example, as being "inspired," it is perhaps misleading to use this English word to translate Paul's dynamic Greek word *theopneustos.* This word contains two elements: *theo,* which means "God"; and *pneu-,* which means "breath." Thus the word means: "That which is breathed out by God." This word then affirms clearly that the Scriptures originate in God himself. The figure of breathing brings attention to the mouth. "From my mouth has gone forth a word," God says (Is. 45:23). Paul obviously thought that what Scripture says, God says.

Application
1/List all the purposes suggested in 2 Timothy 3:10—4:5 for reading and studying the Bible. How does the Bible serve these purposes in your life?

_____

_____

_____

_____

Further Study
1/Paul's testimony to Scripture refers specifically to what we call the Old Testament. Compare what Paul claims for his own words: 1 Corinthians 2:13; 14:37; 1 Thessalonians 2:13. Then recall what Peter said about Paul's writing, 2 Peter 3:15-16.
2/See pp. 30-36 of *In Understanding Be Men* by T. C. Hammond (IVP, 1968).
3/Some object that the view of Scripture stated here amounts to an assertion that God dictated Scripture and the men who wrote it were like mechanical dictaphones. They reject and ridicule a "dictation" theory of inspiration, pointing to the evidence of human, stylistic differences among the writers. What do you think? Study the following Old Testament statements to see how the writers experienced their inspiration and viewed their writing: Exodus 24:3-8; 2 Samuel 23:1-4; 1 Chronicles 29:29-30; Ezra 1:1; Isaiah 1:1-20; Jeremiah 1:1-4, 9; 13:1-9; 30:1-4; 36:1-4; Ezekiel 1:1—3:4; Hosea 1:1-8; Amos 1:1.

study 3
jesus' testimony to scripture (I)

Matthew 15:3-9; 19:3-6; 22:29-32, 41-44

Questions
1/Matthew 15:3-9
Whom does Jesus describe as the source of Moses' laws?

What phrase does Jesus use in verse 6 to describe Moses' commandments?

To whom does Jesus ascribe the quote in verses 8 and 9? Who is the "me" of the quote? What equation is Jesus making about Isaiah's words?

2/Matthew 19:3-6
To whom does Jesus ascribe the quote in verse 5?

See the origin of this quote, Genesis 2:24. Who is the "speaker" of these words?

_____

What is the significance of the fact that Jesus ascribes directly to God what is simple narrative in Genesis?

_____

_____

3/Matthew 22:29-32, 41-44
What do you understand about Jesus' view of Scripture from the way that he makes his argument depend on the tense of a single verb in verse 32?

_____

_____

What does Jesus indicate about the source of Scripture in verse 43?

_____

In these exchanges, what does Jesus' use of Scripture imply about his attitude toward its authority for deciding doctrinal questions?

_____

_____

_____

Comments

In these incidents, Jesus did not state directly his opinion of Scripture. His opinion becomes evident incidentally to some other point that he made. This incidental nature of his remarks makes them the more impressive because it shows that Jesus assumed as true the kind of view that Peter and Paul enunciated. For Jesus the Scriptures were God's word spoken through men, accurate even to the minutest detail. What the Old Testament writers were saying, God was saying, because they were speaking "in the Spirit." This appears in his saying that God said the words of the writer of Genesis, even though they were not attributed to God. It appears in his arguing about God's relationship to Abraham, Isaac and Jacob. The core of that argument is that since God, speaking four hundred years after Abraham had died, said "I *am* the God of Abraham," then Abraham must not have ceased to exist upon his physical death.

Douglas Johnson declared: "He who desires to live in the spirit of the New Testament must make it his aim to find and to follow the mind of Christ. It is a flagrant misnomer for a man to call himself a true Christian and then to decline obedience to what is clearly Christ's teaching on any given matter." (*The Christian and His Bible,* IVP, 1953, p. 72)

Application

1/What example worthy of your following do you see in Jesus in this study?

Further Study

1/Study the following to see more of Jesus' testimony about Scripture: Luke 16:17; 24:13-27, 45-48. Compare Matthew 15:4 with Mark 7:10; what does the difference indicate?

study 4
jesus' testimony to scripture (II)

John 10:24-39

Questions

1/What can you tell about the people to whom Jesus is talking?

_____

_____

2/Why was the threat made on Jesus' life?

_____

3/In verses 34 and 35, Jesus quotes from the Old Testament. What does Jesus call the source of his quotation?

_____

The quote is actually from Psalm 82:6. What is significant about this?

_____

_____

4/On what one word in the quote does Jesus' argument hinge? What is significant about this?

_____

_____

5/What does Jesus affirm directly about the Scripture? What does this mean?

_____

_____

_____

Comments

"The Scripture cannot be broken." This is the most forthright testimony that Jesus gives about Scripture. The word *broken* in relationship to a law or principle implies to violate or to make ineffective. Jesus thus affirms the absolute authority of the Scripture; it is like a law which is unbreakable, something like the "law of gravity," rather than a "speed law."

When Jesus was threatened by a Jewish lynch-mob, he based his appeal on the Scripture which they believed and asserted "cannot be broken." Its words stand as a sure, trustworthy standard of what we should believe and what we should do. Jesus confidently bases his argument on a single word of the Scripture.

Application

1/List the claims that Jesus makes about himself here. Concentrate on the truth of each as you worship him.

_____

_____

_____

2/What does it mean for you to be one of Jesus' sheep? How would this relationship affect your attitude toward the Scripture?

_____

_____

Further Study

1/Identify Jesus' view of the Scripture as shown in Matthew 5:18 and Luke 16:17; compare it with that studied here.

2/Our argument for the inspiration of the Bible, thus far, goes like this: (1) the Bible's writers claim that their words come from God; (2) the Gospel accounts, considered simply as historical sources, show that Jesus held this same view, that the words of Scripture are the words of God; (3) thus, the person who calls Jesus "Lord" will acknowledge the Bible as being truly God's Word.

Two matters must be considered in order to make this argument complete. First, some have suggested that Jesus merely adopted the view held by his audience, for the sake of the argument. He accommodated himself to their assumptions. What do you think of this? Second, when Jesus spoke of the Scripture, he, of course, referred to the Old Testament only. Does Jesus' testimony to the authority of Scripture extend to the New Testament? For a discussion of his statements regarding the teaching of the apostles, see chapter 5 in _Christ and the Bible_ by John Wenham (IVP, 1972).

study 5
jesus' attitude toward scripture

Matthew 4:1-11

Questions

1/Diagram the story by completing the following chart:

	1st challenge	2nd challenge	3rd challenge
a. suggestion by the tempter	_____	_____	_____
b. natural desire to which suggestion appealed	_____	_____	_____
c. Jesus' answer	_____	_____	_____
d. the sin that Jesus would have committed had he complied	_____	_____	_____

2/Why did Jesus quote Scripture in answer to each temptation?

3/Compare verse 6 with verses 4, 7 and 10. What two different ways of treating Scripture are illustrated? How did the devil pervert the Scripture?

Comments

When Martin Luther was on trial for heresy, he boldly replied: "Unless I am convinced by the testimony of the Scripture or by clear reason, I am bound by the Scripture I have quoted and my conscience is captive to the Word of God. I cannot and I will not recant any word I have spoken." The attitude of the great reformer we must surely find commendable. For we can see that these words reflect Jesus' attitude toward Scripture. His thoughts and actions were held captive by God's Word.

The devil appealed to legitimate desires and goals in each temptation. It would not be real temptation if it did not appeal to real desires. The reason that Jesus could not follow the devil's advice was that he moved at the command of only One: God. He lived, in the first place, by every word that comes out of the mouth of God. To have done what the devil told him to do would have been to unbind himself from the Word of God and thus to act independently from God.

There is a difference between using Scripture for your own ends, and being bound by Scripture. In the former, you actually place yourself above the Bible and manipulate it to prove your point or accomplish your purposes. The devil's use of the Scripture in verse 6 illustrates this. But Jesus acted in the opposite fashion; he placed himself under the authority of God's Word.

Application

1/What worthy examples to follow do you discover in this incident?

2/How might you think and act in a way that is more like the devil's pattern than Jesus'? Can you find an incident in your life where you have let Scripture rule your action rather than trying to manipulate Scripture to your own goals?

Further Study

1/Additional understanding of this story can be gained by studying the Old Testament context from which the quotations came, Deuteronomy 8:3; 6:13; 6:16; Psalm 91:11-12. What might be suggested by the fact that Jesus quoted from the same Old Testament book each time?

John 5:37-41; Psalm 119:1-16

Questions

1/John 5:37-41. What does Jesus say about the relationship between himself and the Scriptures?

_____

_____

2/What does Jesus indicate about the right and wrong ways to approach Scripture?

_____

_____

_____

3/Psalm 119:1-16. In every verse of the first two stanzas of the psalm, David makes a reference to Scripture. List all the words that David uses. Then write a brief descriptive definition of each of these words, telling what each indicates about Scripture.

_____

_____

_____

_____

_____

_____

_____

_____

4/List the words that David uses to show what he has done or will do with respect to the content of Scripture.

_____

_____

_____

_____

Comment
There is a quality of life that God desires a Christian to have. It is a life that is saturated with his Word. It is a life that instinctively responds to situations with a mindset that is molded and informed by God's view of things. This quality is not natural to us, nor can we achieve it by casual consultation of Scripture. It will not become ours if we do not diligently pursue it. Only when we seek God with our whole heart can his Word become for us what it was for Jesus—

the living guide for life.

The Bible is not merely a textbook for right doctrine; it is not merely a handbook of right living; it is not even merely the fountain of salvation. It is the revelation of a Person. Through it we may have the mind of Christ (1 Cor. 2: 14-16), speak his Word and live out his life. In this way we reflect the glory of God. The decisive test of our view of the Bible is not how we state our belief about it, but how God's Word saturates our whole being.

Application
1/How can you respond to God's Word in the various ways that David said he did? Think through the list you made in question 4.

_____

_____

_____

2/Do you find Jesus Christ in your study of Scripture and does it lead you to him? If yes, praise and thank him for it. If no, ask him to help you.

Further Study
1/John R. W. Stott states concisely the line of reasoning this guide has followed with respect to Scripture in his booklet *The Authority of the Bible* (IVP).
2/*In Understanding Be Men*, pp. 38-40.

summary

Write concise responses to the following:

1/This is what I believe about the Bible:

_____

_____

_____

_____

_____

2/This is the impact that belief has on my life:

_____

_____

_____

_____

3/These are my questions about the Bible:

_____

_____

_____

_____

_____

"The deity of our
Lord Jesus Christ."

The key word in this statement is *deity*. The statement affirms that the quality of "deity" belongs to the man, Jesus, who lived two thousand years ago in the land of Palestine. Leon Morris has well observed that "deity is not an easy term to define." But in describing what that term intends to designate, Morris has suggested helpfully:

It is not impossible to imagine a line which separates God from all God's creatures, so that on one side is God, and on the other is everything less than God. If we ask on which side of this line Jesus Christ is to be found, the answer given by all the New Testament writers is 'God's side.' (The Lord from Heaven, *InterVarsity Press, p. 107.*)

In the approach to Christian doctrine taken in this guide, the belief concerning the deity of Jesus is logically prior to all other doctrine. First, considering the historical data surrounding the life of the man, Jesus of Nazareth, we are driven to the conclusion that he thought he was God. Second, faced with this self-concept of Jesus, we must decide whether he was right. If we decide that he was not correct in his opinion of himself, Christianity crumbles to the ground, and, of course, Christian doctrine is a useless matter. But if we decide that Jesus was correct in that opinion, we can begin to erect the structure of Christian doctrine on the basis of his teaching which, as was exemplified in topic A, leads us to affirm "the unique divine inspiration, entire trustworthiness and authority of the Bible." Though the deity of Jesus *is* logically prior to the authority and inspiration of Scripture, this guide deals first with Scripture simply because it comes first in the IVCF statement of faith.

study 1
jesus' self-concept

John 5:1-29

Questions

1/How long had the man been ill? What importance does this have to the healing action?

2/Why did Jesus ask him if he wanted to be healed? What does this show about Jesus?

3/When the Jews objected to Jesus' act, what was his reply? State the meaning of this in your own words.

4/What specifically offended the Jews and caused Jesus to make his long statement?

5/Jesus makes several statements about the relationship of the Son and the Father. Set these into the following chart so that the relationship will be diagrammatically represented.

	About the Father	About the Son
verse 19	_____	_____
verse 21	_____	_____
verse 22	_____	_____
verse 23a	_____	_____
verse 23b	_____	_____
verse 26	_____	_____

Comments

The One whom Jesus called Father was the One the Jews called their God. The Jews understood correctly that when Jesus referred to God as his Father, he was claiming to be equal with God. When they raised that objection, Jesus did not attempt to correct them; rather he showed them how he understood such equality. If Jesus claimed to be equal with the Jews' God, the question arises: What is the relationship between Jesus and the Jews' God? One possible relationship would be that the two were exactly, precisely the same divine person. But Jesus does not say that. There are two distinct personalities involved. (Here is the basis for the Christian doctrine of the Trinity.) Well, then, is one worthy of more honor than the other? No, says Jesus. Instead, he says, whatever honor is thought to be appropriate for the

Father is equally appropriate for Jesus, the Son.

Here is the crux of Jesus' self-concept. It is as if Jesus said: "Think of what is true for you about God; think of how you consider he should be treated. Then apply those thoughts to me and you will be thinking rightly of me." No more positive claim to deity could be given by any person.

Application

1/What is the one response that Jesus says is appropriate to his claim and teaching?

———————————————————————

———————————————————————

2/Consider Jesus' respect for the sick man (v. 6). How could you find an example here to be followed in your life?

———————————————————————

———————————————————————

———————————————————————

3/How can you get others to consider the ideas studied today?

———————————————————————

———————————————————————

Further Study

1/Christianity is the only one of the religions of the world that stands or falls on the identity of its founder: How is this statement true?

2/Study carefully "The Claims of Christ," chapter 2 of *Basic Christianity*, John R. W. Stott (IVP).

3/See John W. Montgomery, *History and Christianity* (IVP, 1964).

topic b
JESUS CHRIST

study 2
who is he?

John 7:1-52

Questions

1/In this chapter, many people's opinions about Jesus
emerge. As you read through the chapter, fill in the following chart:

verse	characters	opinions about Jesus	reason for opinion (where given)

_____

_____

_____

2/Review your list in the third column. Group the opinions into categories of similar notions and label each category.

_____

_____

_____

_____

3/What can you tell about Jesus from this chapter?

_____

_____

_____

4/What does Jesus promise to do for the person who believes in him? What is the significance of this claim?

_____

_____

_____

Comments

When a man claims equality with God, as Jesus did, there is a limited number of conclusions to which we can come logically, once we have understood the claim. We may believe such a claim. If we do not, it is because we have concluded that (1) the idea is preposterous; or (2) the man is deranged; or (3) the man is a deliberate deceiver, or (4) the idea is inconvenient to personal interests or prejudices. These conclusions are all illustrated here. That Jesus' contemporaries came to these conclusions demonstrates the validity of C. S. Lewis' classic paragraph:

A man who was merely a man and said the sort of things Jesus said would not be a great moral teacher. He would either be a lunatic—on a level with the man who says he is a poached egg—or else he would be the Devil of Hell. You must make your choice. Either this man was, and is, the Son of God: or else a madman or something worse. You can shut Him up for a fool, you can spit at Him and kill Him as a demon; or you can fall at His feet and call Him Lord and God. But let us not come with any patronising nonsense about His being a great human teacher. He has not left that open to us. He did not intend to. (Mere Christianity, *New York: Macmillan, 1960, p. 46*)

Application

1/If you had been in Jerusalem on this day, how would you have made up your mind about Jesus?

2/How do you experience the living water that Jesus gives?

Further Study

1/See *Mere Christianity* by C. S. Lewis, especially the chapter "The Shocking Alternative."

2/Read IVP's evangelistic booklet, *Have You Considered Him?* by Wilbur Smith.

3/Some of those who refused to believe Jesus' claim based their opinion on their analysis of Scripture (compare Mt. 2:1-8, 22-23; Mic. 5:2; Ps. 89:3-4). What lesson can you see in this?

4/Read *I Came to Set the Earth on Fire* by R. T. France (IVP, 1975).

study 3
peter's confession

Luke 9:18-36

Questions

1/Why, do you think, did Jesus ask these questions?

_____

_____

2/Who did Peter say Jesus was? What does this mean?
(Compare the statement with its parallel in Mt. 16:16.)

_____

_____

_____

3/After Peter's acknowledgment of who Jesus was, what two
subjects does Jesus insert into the conversation (vv. 22-23)?
Why are these introduced _after_ Peter's acknowledgment?

_____

_____

4/List specifically what Jesus requires of the person who would follow him.

_____

_____

_____

5/What do you consider to be the significant items in the story of Jesus' transfiguration? What is their significance?

_____

_____

_____

_____

Comments

For many months the disciples had lived with Jesus. Throughout that time, Jesus' identity gradually had become clearer to them. They had heard him make claims regarding his deity. They had seen his miracles. They had heard his teaching. Now the test had come: to what conclusion had all their observations led them? Peter put it in words: "You are the Messiah, the Son of God."

There are two important facts associated with the disciples' conclusion. Jesus stated, in Matthew's record of this interview, that this conclusion cannot be reached as a sure personal conviction unless God works in a person in a special way so that he believes. Second, this objective conclusion has subjective consequences. If a person concludes that Jesus is deity, then Jesus' claim comes directly and personally: "Follow me." It follows as a reasonable consequence that when one believes Jesus' claim about who he is, he must acknowledge Jesus' claim on his own life.

Application

1/How do you fulfill the requirements that Jesus makes upon his true followers?

_____

_____

_____

2/Write a statement praising Jesus based upon this incident. Begin: "I praise you, Jesus, because you

_____

_____

_____

Further Study

1/This section gives four designations for Jesus in addition to his personal name: "The Christ," "the Son of man," "master," "my Son." What do these names mean and what does each reveal about Jesus? Consult the following: Matthew 1:21; 16:27-28; 21:9; 26:63-65; Luke 4:17-21; John 4:25-42; 12:34; Jeremiah 23:5-6; Daniel 7:13-14.

2/Why does Jesus call himself "Son of man" much more often than "Son of God"?

3/Read *The Lord from Heaven* by Leon Morris (IVP, 1974).

study 4
the bread of life

John 6:25-51

Questions

1/In verse 28 what question do the people ask Jesus? Why did they ask this?

_____

_____

_____

2/What change did Jesus make in their wording when he answered? What does this signify?

_____

_____

_____

3/How did the real desire of the people differ from what Jesus wanted for them to desire?

_____

4/List the purpose and uses of bread, as you understand them. How do these give meaning to Jesus' claim: "I am the bread of life"?

5/Jesus gives two results of believing in him (vv. 35, 40). What is the difference between these?

6/How does Jesus explain the failure of the people to believe in him (36-40) or to understand who he is (42-44)?

Comments
There is a strange tension in this section of Scripture. When the people come to Jesus wishing to have more free food,

he wants to convince them to be less concerned about physical hunger and more concerned about spiritual nutrition. Jesus tells them to pay attention to their spiritual needs as they pay attention to their stomachs. But when they do not do as he says, Jesus declares that they could not do it anyway. Their unbelief testifies that they were not prepared to believe in Jesus.

Here is the point: The fact that Jesus is deity is a truth for which there is adequate reason to believe. Logically, when faced with the evidence, a person should believe in Jesus. But many do not, because only those who are taught by God, drawn by God, given to Jesus by God can understand who Jesus is and thus believe in him.

Application
1/State specifically the ways in which you experience Jesus satisfying your hungers.

_____

_____

_____

2/What manifestations of hunger and thirst do you see in people around you? How can Jesus meet these needs? How can you bring the bread of life to these people?

_____

_____

_____

_____

3/What kind of prayer for non-Christians is appropriate on the basis of Jesus' words here?

Further Study

1/What in this study assures us that a person cannot become a Christian by rational argument alone, that a person cannot be argued into receiving Jesus Christ, that if anyone only knew the facts adequately he would still not necessarily be a Christian? How should this influence the way in which a Christian deals with a non-Christian? What role, then does apologetics play? (See also 1 Pet. 3:15 and 2 Tim. 2:24-26.)

study 5
jesus' gospel

Hebrews 1:1—2:4

Questions

1/Verses 1 and 2 contain three pairs of contrasting items. List them and tell their significance.

_____

_____

_____

_____

_____

_____

2/Summarize what verses 2-4 tell about the Son's:

person:

_____

_____

work:

_____

_____

position:

_____

_____

3/What is the principal contrast in this chapter?

_____

What things are true of the Son that are not true of angels?

_____

_____

_____

4/By what names is the Son addressed in verses 8 and 10? What is the significance of these names?

_____

_____

5/Who are the three witnesses of the message of great salvation? Why should we pay close attention to that message?

Comments

This section asserts the deity of Jesus Christ in bold terms.
God, because he is love, communicates himself to people.
He did this in different times and in different ways; but he
did it supremely by becoming one of us. This is the gospel,
the message of great salvation through Jesus Christ.

In Jesus of Nazareth, God's greatest word is spoken.
Jesus' message is more important than that of prophets or
angels because there is a difference of quality between him
and the other messengers. They were merely carriers of
a message; he "reflects the glory of God and bears the very
stamp of his nature," (v. 3) or, as Phillips translates, he is
"the flawless expression of the nature of God." He is the
message as well as the messenger.

The full deity of Jesus Christ is affirmed by the command
to worship him—none is to be worshiped except God—and
by the forms of address chosen for him—God and Lord.
In calling Jesus "Lord" in Hebrews 1:10 (a quote from
Ps. 102) and 2:3, the writer gave to him the personal name
of the God of the Old Testament. Since God has communi-
cated himself in this way, to neglect his message must have
frightful consequences.

Application

1/How could you, perhaps, "neglect such a great salvation"? (Note that the writer addresses Christians, "we.") How will you avoid neglecting Jesus' message?

_____

_____

_____

2/Worship Jesus, specifically, through meditating on what is stated about him here.

Further Study

1/There have always been persons calling themselves Christians who have argued that while Jesus was divine (in some way), he was not fully God, essentially equal with God the Father. Can you think of some people who assert this? How would you demonstrate that the New Testament portrayal of Jesus is correctly specified in the words of the Nicene Creed: "[Jesus Christ is] God of God, True God of True God . . . of one substance with the Father"?

2/*In Understanding Be Men,* pp. 99-107.

3/Using your answer to question 2 (p. 48) as an outline, write a paragraph statement of the gospel in your own words.

study 6
christ's position

Ephesians 1:3-23

Questions

1/In verses 3-14, at least ten things are mentioned that God has done for us in Christ. List as many as you can.

_____

_____

_____

_____

_____

_____

2/What reasons are given here for God's sending the Son to earth as a human being? For how long had this been planned?

_____

_____

_____

_____

_____

3/In verses 20-23, Paul states three features of the position which God gave to Christ. Identify them and state their meaning.

_____

_____

_____

_____

4/Paul speaks of two inheritances, one belonging to believers (v. 14) and the other to God (v. 18). Describe each.

_____

_____

_____

_____

_____

Comments
The appropriate questions to ask when we realize that God was a man in Jesus Christ are, Why did that occur and what difference does it make? Paul shows here that it was part of an eternal plan arranged by God. That plan was designed,

first and foremost, so that God's glory will be praised (vv. 6, 12, 14). That plan culminates in the unification of all things in Christ (v. 10), so that Christ will be supreme Lord over all things.

One chief problem stands in the way of that supremacy: Human beings are in revolt against God. In sending Christ to earth and raising him from death, God proclaimed his desire that all people yield to Christ's authority. And, through Jesus' death (v. 7), God made it possible for people to call off their revolt and to proclaim, "Jesus is Lord." That is, Jesus Christ is the sovereign of the universe and the head of the church. He has been given "the name which is above every name, that at the name of Jesus every knee should bow, in heaven and on earth and under the earth, and every tongue confess that Jesus Christ is Lord, to the glory of God the Father" (Phil. 2:9-11).

Application
1/Go over your list in question 3 and thank God for each item, stating what each means for you.

_____

_____

2/How can you appropriately acknowledge Christ's position now?

_____

_____

3/Pray for yourself and your friends Paul's prayer for his readers. How might you expect God to answer this prayer?

_____

Further Study

1/Other guides for study of Jesus Christ, published by InterVarsity Press are: *Discovering the Gospel of Mark; Discussions on the Life of Jesus Christ; Jesus the Disciple Maker; Getting to Know Jesus.*

2/Keep this study in the front of your mind as you go through the remaining studies in this guide. It is an introduction to them.

topic b
JESUS CHRIST

summary

Write concise responses to the following:

1/This is what I believe about Jesus Christ:

_____

_____

_____

_____

_____

2/This is the impact that belief has on my life:

_____

_____

_____

_____

3/These are my questions about Jesus Christ:

_____

_____

_____

_____

_____

topic c
JESUS' DEATH AND RESURRECTION

"The necessity and efficacy
of the substitutionary death
of Jesus Christ
for the redemption of the world,
and the historic fact
of his bodily resurrection."

God invaded history bodily in Jesus of Nazareth. In becoming human, God showed a lot about himself and his truth. But this invasion was more than a demonstration. God the Son came "to give his life as a ransom for many" (Mt. 20:28). The picture of a ransom appears in our statement in the words "substitutionary" and "redemption." By his death, Jesus Christ bore in our place the penalty of God's judgment against sin, so that we could be excused from that penalty.

The purpose of Jesus' coming to earth was not completed with his death, however. Three days after Jesus' death, his friends discovered that the cave in which he had been buried no longer contained the body, and within hours they were walking, talking and eating with him again. Jesus Christ was raised from death.

With the doctrine of Jesus' death and resurrection, we come to the heart of the message of the Bible, declared from its beginning to its end. It is the eternal plan mentioned in the previous study. Six studies can only include the barest sample of the Bible's teaching about it. These studies will focus on aspects of Jesus' death and resurrection that have been disputed by modern thinkers and therefore emphasized by evangelical Christians.

**study 1
sin and death**

Romans 5:6—6:4

Questions

1/What facts about people emphasize Christ's death as the primary evidence of God's love?

_____

_____

_____

_____

_____

2/List the words by which Paul expresses what Jesus' death accomplished for us.

_____

_____

_____

3/What is the relationship between sin and death?

_____

_____

_____

4/Verses 12-19 contain an extended contrast. List the contrasting elements that Paul states.

_____

_____

_____

_____

_____

_____

5/What direct effect should Jesus' death have on the conduct of the Christian believer?

_____

_____

Comments

Paul shows here both the necessity and the efficacy of Jesus' death. It was necessary that Jesus die for sinful human beings because apart from his death, all people stand under the penalty and power of death (v. 12). Jesus' death was efficacious (it worked) because God accepts

Jesus' death as full payment of that penalty and it breaks that power which death held over people (v. 18).

Paul begins with the premise of the connection between sin and death. Sin entails death as its consequence (Rom. 6:23). God warned Adam of this (Gen. 2:17); but Adam sinned. Then Paul notes that all descendants of Adam died, even though they did not perform the same act of sin (eating the fruit) that Adam did. This must mean, Paul reasons, that Adam's sin implicated all his progeny, making them all subject to the power of death. The link between sin and the sinner's death was broken by God's act of love in Jesus Christ's death for us. We were helpless to break it for ourselves. But because of Jesus' death, we can have life.

Application

1/Why and how do you rejoice (v. 11) because of the death of Jesus?

_____

_____

2/In what ways do you "walk in newness of life"? How may you do so today?

_____

_____

_____

Further Study

1/*In Understanding Be Men,* pp. 121-133.

2/Read *Go Free! The Meaning of Justification* by Robert M. Horn (IVP, 1976).

3/Become acquainted with an evangelical classic of Jesus' death, *The Death of Christ* by James Denney (IVP). Though out of print, it is fortunately still available in an occasional bookstore or library.

Leviticus 16:1-34

Questions

1/Verses 1-5: What procedures were prescribed for the high priest (Aaron) for this special day of the year? What adjective occurs four times in this paragraph, indicating the lesson God is teaching about himself in these instructions?

_____

_____

_____

_____

2/Verses 6-14: What was accomplished with the bull that the high priest killed?

_____

_____

3/Verses 15-19: What was accomplished with the goat that was killed?

_____

_____

_____

4/Verses 20-22: What was accomplished and signified with the goat that was turned loose?

_____

_____

5/Verses 29-34: What instructions are given about this special day?

_____

_____

_____

6/What do you consider to be the principal lessons of this chapter

about God?

_____

_____

about man?

_____

_____

about sin?

_____

_____

Comments

The word *atonement* derives from the process indicated literally by its component words: the condition of being "at one." How can God and man be brought to oneness, to a reconciliation? In the ceremony of atonement, God depicts the way that it can be done. First, he shows his demands of holiness; God can be at one only with what is holy, because he is holy. Second, he shows the serious consequences of sin. As Isaiah put it: "Your iniquities have made a separation between you and your God and your sins have hid his face from you." Man and God cannot be at one until sin is removed. Third, God shows that only through death can sin be removed. "I have given it [blood] for you upon the altar to make atonement for your souls; for it is the blood that makes atonement" (Lev. 17:11). Fourth, God shows how a substitute for a person can accomplish atonement.

This study of Jewish atonement is necessary for an understanding of the New Testament teaching about Jesus' death because, first, God gave the Hebrews their ritual to prefigure the work of Jesus and, second, the early Christians' understanding of Jesus' death grew out of the context of the Jewish religion. Thus, with this study we are prepared for the next two studies in the book of Hebrews.

Application

1/What attributes of God are portrayed in this study? Worship him for them.

_____

2/What difference for your life is made by the fact that God is holy? (See 1 Pet. 1:14-19.)

Further Study

1/See "Atonement" and "Atonement, Day of" in the *New Bible Dictionary* (IVP).
2/See the incident to which verse 1 refers—Leviticus 10:1-3. What lesson does God teach through this?
3/Read Edith Schaeffer's *Christianity is Jewish* (Tyndale, 1975).

study 3
christian atonement

Hebrews 9:1-28

Questions

1/According to the writer, what was the purpose of the Jewish system of the old covenant?

2/What are the limitations of the old system?

3/What is the significance of the designation given of Christ in verse 11?

4/What results follow from the shedding of bulls' and goats' blood? How does this compare with the effects of Christ's Blood?

5/How do verses 15-18 indicate the necessity of Jesus' dying?

6/What is the chief evidence that the efficacy of Jesus' death is infinitely greater than the deaths of bulls and goats?

Comments

The atonement of the Hebrew system enables us to understand Jesus' death. That system illustrated (1) that a holy God demands a purification from sin of all persons who desire to approach him, (2) that a death is required so that the benefits of God's promise may be realized, (3) that blood must be shed for there to be any forgiveness of sin. The seriousness with which God views sin is underscored in all of this. Any treatment of Jesus' death which fails to see in it God's great sacrifice for sin is not taking seriously the greatness of the holiness of God.

But if the holiness of God is great, his grace is greater. The word *covenant* points us to this. It shows that God himself took the initiative in providing forgiveness and making at-one-ness possible. The Greek word translated *covenant* here is not the word that designates an agreement between two persons; it is the word used to designate the will of a testator. Leon Morris pointedly observes: "There is an air of finality about a will. You cannot dicker with a testator. You accept what he leaves you on the condition he lays down, or you reject it." (*The Cross in the New Testament,* Grand Rapids: Eerdmans, 1965, p. 278.)

Application

1/What does verse 14 say is the practical result of Jesus' death? What does this mean in concrete, active terms for your life today?

_____

_____

2/How will you respond to the truth that Christ's death is a one-time event, never to be repeated (v. 28)?

_____

_____

Further Study

1/The view that Jesus' death was substitutionary—his death instead of ours, as a sacrifice—excites repulsion and disgust among many modern writers. They seem to say, "True, the Bible does teach that Jesus died in our place, as a sacrifice, but this idea cannot recommend itself to enlightened minds. The idea of sacrifice is primitive. God's letting one person die for another is immoral." How would you respond if a friend raised this objection to your presentation of the gospel? See Hammond's excellent essay in *In Understanding Be Men,* pp. 121-133.

The objection could also be expressed in Erik Routley's words: "No. No. It wouldn't be good news. I shouldn't permit it for a moment. And if I did, I should be paralysed for the rest of my life with a burden of guilt for letting him do it for me [that is, die in my place]." (*The Man for Others,* New York: Oxford, 1964, p. 84.) What do you think of this?

study 4
results of jesus' death

Hebrews 10:1-25

Questions

1/According to the writer, what did the sacrifices of the Hebrew system really accomplish?

2/What is contrasted here with the "once for all" offering of Jesus' body? (Notice the many contrasts in vv. 10-12.)

3/What did Jesus' death accomplish that the old covenant sacrifices never could?

Comments

The Jewish sacrifices gave an illustration of God's way of treating sin. But they had a serious shortcoming which was also illustrated in the Old Testament system. Those sacrifices did not really take away sins, and thus they were repeated as a continual reminder of sin. Accordingly, the way into God's presence, symbolized by the inner tent (Heb. 9:6-8), was barred to the people. Until Christ's death "opened for us a way through the curtain" (see Mt. 27:50-51), there was no access to God's presence.

But the situation has been changed. Jesus' death truly and effectively dealt with sin. The power of sin was broken. Now we can have confidence before God, but only "by the blood of Jesus." That blood declared two truths at the same time: God's holiness and his mercy. Because he is holy, we cannot come to God without the blood; we have the blood only because God, rich in mercy, gave it to us.

Application

1/The writer draws several applications from his doctrine. What should be your attitude toward God?

_____

_____

What should be your action toward God?

_____

_____

What should be your attitude and action toward other

Christians?

_____

_____

2/How can the truths disclosed here influence your thinking during the time when you are participating in the Lord's Supper (Holy Communion)?

_____

_____

_____

Further Study

1/Study the following verses and discover what each indicates about the application of Jesus' death to you: 2 Timothy 2:11; Galatians 2:20; Colossians 2:12-15; Romans 8:17; Galatians 5:24; 6:14.

2/It might legitimately be asked, Did Jesus view his death in the same way that we have discussed it in this study? What is the importance of this question? Study Matthew 26:26-29 in this regard. See "Jesus' View of His Death," *Getting to Know Jesus* (IVP), pp. 62-64.

3/Did God deceive the Jews if the old covenant sacrifices could never take away sins? How was access to personal relationship with God achieved in those times? See John 8:56; Romans 4:1-25; Galatians 3:6-9; Psalm 32:1-5; Psalm 51:6-10, 16-17.

study 5
resurrection as historic fact

1 Corinthians 15:1-19; Luke 24:36-47

Questions

1/What facts does Paul say constitute the "gospel" which he preached?

_____

_____

_____

2/How does Paul emphasize here that Jesus' resurrection was an actual, physical event?

_____

_____

_____

3/What would be the logical consequences if it were not an historical event?

_____

4/What evidence does Luke's account include that Jesus actually arose from death physically?

5/Why did Jesus consider his resurrection to be necessary?

Comments

Paul's primary purpose in writing this section was not to describe or prove Jesus' resurrection, but to refute a false teaching current among the believers at Corinth. This fact makes his point more compelling. Some Christians in Corinth, it appears, were saying that there would be no resurrection in the end time for Christian believers. Paul knew this teaching to be false because he saw that its logical consequence was that Jesus did not really rise. And for Paul, such an idea was unthinkable. No real, physical resurrection of Jesus—no Christian faith. If Jesus did not really rise from the dead, nothing else that Christians claim has any meaning.

Paul acquired this view from Jesus. Jesus saw his physical

return to life as inseparably linked with his death in the plan which God was working out in history. That is why he regularly predicted his resurrection when he spoke of his death (Mt. 16:21; Lk. 18:31-33; Jn. 2:19-22). One was unthinkable without the other. In fact, one time Jesus declared that he was going to die in order that he could rise (Jn. 10:17).

Application
1/Consider what results belief in Jesus' resurrection had for Paul (1 Cor. 15:8-10). How might you follow his example today?

2/Besides his death and resurrection, what else did Jesus see as God's plan (Lk. 24:46-49)? How can you be involved in this?

Further Study
1/Some who call themselves Christians argue that Jesus' resurrection was not a bodily resurrection. They speak of a "spiritual resurrection" by which they mean that in some way the spirit of Jesus lived on after he died and that he continues to exert an influence on Christians. What do you think of this? Is it important now whether we think of Jesus' resurrection primarily in spiritual or physical terms?
2/Jesus found his resurrection foretold in the Old Testament. So did Paul. Where did they find it? Perhaps the following will help: Psalm 16:8-11 (cf. Acts 2:25-32); Isaiah 55:3 (cf. Acts 13:33-37); Isaiah 53:10-12; Jonah 1:17 (cf. Mt. 12:39-40).
3/*Who Moved the Stone?* (IVP, 1958) was written by Frank Morison, a history student who didn't accept the resurrection as historical. His mind was changed during the process of researching the death and resurrection of Jesus. This book records his conclusions.

JESUS' DEATH AND RESURRECTION

study 6
results of jesus' resurrection

1 Corinthians 15:20-57

Questions

1/What has come as a result of Jesus' resurrection (v. 21)? What is the significance of Christ's being "the first fruits"?

_____

_____

_____

2/What assurance is given to us on the basis of Jesus' resurrection regarding the ultimate condition of things (vv. 24-28)?

_____

_____

_____

3/In verses 44-49, Paul contrasts Christ and Adam. List the items of contrast. What is the point of this contrast? Compare with the contrast in study 1.

_____

_____

_____

_____

_____

_____

_____

Comments

Jesus' resurrection is the crucial evidence of his deity. Paul says that he was "designated Son of God in power . . . by his resurrection from the dead" (Rom. 1:4).

But there is more significance to Jesus' resurrection than mere demonstration. His resurrection brings concrete results. That is why there could be no Christianity unless Jesus actually rose. Paul states three of these results here. (1) The resurrection is the accomplishment of a victory by which Jesus Christ becomes ruler, first of the church, and then of all created reality; (2) the resurrection of Jesus makes it possible and sure that we ourselves shall be resurrected in the future and enjoy an unending life; and (3) the resurrection brings life to us in this age. The life of eternity has broken into the present, so that we can achieve victory over sin on the basis of Jesus' victory (Rom. 6:4-14). There is a power available to us now for living the Christian style of life which is ours because of Jesus' resurrection (Phil. 3:8b-11). Because Jesus' death and resurrection have defeated sin and its consequence, death, the Christian can claim this victory for his own life.

Application

1/Ask God to give you a clear, confident awareness of his power at work in you.

2/What can you be doing now to reflect in practice the condition referred to in question 2?

_____

_____

3/How might such ultimate victory affect the way you handle disappointments and setbacks?

_____

_____

Further Study

1/How does this study help you to understand why one of the two conditions for salvation given in Romans 10:9 is belief "that God raised him from the dead"? What does this stipulation have to do with the first condition, confession that "Jesus is Lord"?

2/Imagine that archaeologists have discovered a buried body which can be shown by irrefutable evidence and logic to be that of Jesus. Write a letter to a non-Christian friend expressing your response to this discovery. What would you say about your religious beliefs, your religious experiences, the significance of material facts?

3/_In Understanding Be Men,_ pp. 112-117.

4/"The Resurrection of Jesus Christ," _Getting to Know Jesus_ (IVP, 1973), pp. 79-87.

JESUS' DEATH AND RESURRECTION

summary

Write concise responses to the following:

1/This is what I believe about the death of Jesus:

_____

_____

_____

_____

2/This is what impact that belief has on my life:

_____

_____

_____

_____

3/This is what I believe about the resurrection of Jesus:

_____

_____

_____

_____

4/This is what impact that belief has on my life:

_____

_____

_____

_____

5/These are my questions about Jesus' death and resurrection:

_____

_____

_____

_____

REGENERATION BY THE SPIRIT

"The presence and power
of the Holy Spirit
in the work of
regeneration."

The Holy Spirit is at work in the world bringing about a change in people by which they become children of God, a change so radical that it is a new birth. "Regeneration" literally means "rebirth." Thus "regeneration" refers to the experience of being "born again" which evangelicals have persistently preached. The popular image of evangelicals associates them with this notion probably more than with any other. The conviction that people need to be regenerated drives evangelicals to evangelism which attracts attention to them. They have proclaimed the gospel of salvation in Jesus Christ in a variety of ways, some of which have drawn ridicule, both undeserved and deserved. But ridicule, misunderstanding and mistakes should not cause us to shy away from this important subject.

In studying this topic we shall examine what the Bible teaches about the necessity of regeneration, the way the Holy Spirit carries out the transformation and the way people experience the effects of the Spirit's activity in rebirth. The result of this change is the greatest thing a human being can experience. He becomes a child of God (Jn. 1:12-13) and a brother of Jesus Christ (Rom. 8:17; Heb. 2:11).

study 1
jesus talks about regeneration

John 3:1-12

Questions

1/List all the things you can tell about Nicodemus from this section. (Then see what else you can learn from Jn. 7:50-51; 19:39.)

2/Who does Nicodemus think Jesus is? Why?

3/Jesus' answer to Nicodemus in verse 3 sometimes strikes people as being unrelated to Nicodemus' statement in verse 2. That his statement really does follow on Nicodemus' confession is evident only when the phrases "born again" and "kingdom of God" are understood.

What is it to be "born again"? List all you can discover in this section about this concept. Then refer to the following: John 1:12-13; 1 Peter 1:3, 23; James 1:18.

_____

_____

_____

_____

What is the "kingdom of God"? Consider, first, what a kingdom is. Consult the following passages to develop your own definition of the kingdom of God: Luke 11:20; 17:20-21; 9:27; John 18:36; Mark 10:14; 12:34.

_____

_____

_____

_____

_____

What elements common both to "born again" and "kingdom of God" did you find?

_____

_____

_____

4/How is a person "born again"? What is the point that Jesus makes by referring to the wind?

_____

_____

_____

5/What is Nicodemus' problem with what Jesus tells him?

_____

_____

Comments

Jesus' discussion with Nicodemus is the definitive scriptural statement regarding the Holy Spirit's work of regeneration. Jesus declares outright that a regeneration is necessary before a person partakes of the life of God and experiences God's sphere of rule. In making this statement, Jesus implies that all persons are naturally outside of God's kingdom and that only those who are born again as the result of God's will and action become citizens of God's kingdom.

Jesus does not command Nicodemus to be born again. He states the simple fact that without rebirth a person does not experience God's kingdom, that is, God's direct rule over him. But when a person has been born again, he can see God at work around him. He can realize that Jesus really is the Son of God. Rebirth brings a new way of seeing things and makes spiritual truths understandable.

Application

1/If you have been born again, how can you now live to show that you are a citizen of a kingdom of which others around you are not citizens? How can you acknowledge God's kingship in your life today? (Col. 1:9-14 and 1 Pet. 2: 9-10 may help you to be practical in your answer.)

_____

_____

_____

2/Nicodemus' understanding of things Jesus talked about was limited because Jesus spoke about things beyond Nicodemus' ordinary experience—"heavenly things." Many things we study in Scripture are likewise difficult to understand because they are "heavenly things." They can be understood only by the aid of the Holy Spirit (1 Cor. 2:9-16). Always ask for the Spirit's guidance when you study the Bible.

Further Study

1/*In Understanding Be Men*, pp. 146-147.

2/Read chapter 5 of *The Way of Holiness* (IVP, 1967) by K. F. W. Prior, especially pp. 36-38, and chapter 6. (This book is out of print, but is still available in bookstores and libraries.)

3/See "regeneration" in the *New Bible Dictionary* (Eerdmans, 1962).

Ephesians 2:1-10

Questions

1/Paul describes the condition of his readers before they became Christians in at least six ways. List these.

2/What is the meaning of "by nature" (v. 3)? (Compare its use in Gal. 4:8.) What does this show about the condition of people?

3/Summarize concisely in your own words what Paul says about those who have not been regenerated ("made alive").

4/How were Paul's readers "made alive"? (This is stated in different ways in vv. 1, 4-6, 8.)

Comments

When we understand what Paul says here about the condition that people are in naturally, we see clearly why Jesus said that everyone had to be born again if he were to experience a relationship with God. Paul paints a dismal and frightening picture of the condition of his readers before they were regenerated. His conclusion: They were dead; they were controlled by Satan; they lived according to their selfish desires and, by their very nature, were subject to God's infinite displeasure.

This picture is one of hopelessness. It would be shameful enough to commit some sins against the holy God. Having committed just a few sins, we should be afraid to face him. But we might still think that we could do something about a few sins to set the ledger straight. Not so. The human condition is more serious than that. By their very nature, human beings provoke God's judgment against them. The situation is hopeless—except for two tremendous words: "But God." A human being is naturally dead. He cannot do a thing to set himself right with God. A dead horse cannot run. An unregenerate person cannot do a thing to please God (Rom. 8:8). That is why he needs regeneration by God the Holy Spirit. For what a person cannot do for himself, God can do for him. While he is dead and helpless, God will bring spiritual life to him by the same power that brought life to Jesus Christ after his death (Eph. 1:19-20).

Application

1/According to verse 7, what is the reason that God regenerates anyone? How can you begin the fulfillment of this purpose now?

2/What good works (v. 10) has God chosen for you for today?

Further Study

1/Man's natural state of death has far reaching consequences for evangelism. J. I. Packer points out that the consequence is that "unless there is some other factor in the situation, over and above our own endeavours, all evangelistic action is foredoomed to failure." Read pages 106-113 in his *Evangelism and the Sovereignty of God* (IVP, 1961) to see his resolution of this difficulty.

2/How would the view of human nature shown here affect one's attitude toward human institutions such as government, social and economic systems, the social sciences? For a good discussion of this question in the social-political dimension, read chapter 2, "The Nature of Man," in *The Unraveling of America* (IVP, 1974) by Stephen Monsma.

topic d
REGENERATION BY THE SPIRIT

study 3
the beginning

John 15:26—16:15

Questions
1/Why does Jesus think it is to his followers' advantage for him to go away?

_____

_____

_____

2/Jesus states and then expands upon three things of which the Spirit will convince the world. List these and write a paraphrase of each of the ideas for yourself.

_____

_____

_____

_____

_____

3/What is the advantage to Jesus' followers of this convincing work by the Spirit?

4/What is the subject of the Spirit's message of witness?

5/Why is the warning about persecution spoken with the same breath as Jesus' promises about the Spirit's coming? What is the connection?

Comments

Although the Holy Spirit was not specifically mentioned in the Scripture of study 2, we know from other parts of Scripture (for example, study 1) that he is the agent of regeneration. In this passage we see one aspect of his work—the initial stage of his action in people. This is the work of conviction, that is, working in people's minds so they recognize that they need to be reconciled with God. In doing this the Holy Spirit convinces them "of sin and of righteousness and of judgment."

As a person changes from being a "child of disobedience" to a "child of God," he sees three things. First, he sees that sin rules in his life and that apart from believing in Jesus Christ he remains in his sin. So Jesus says that the Spirit convinces a person of his sin by showing him his failure to believe in the Lord Jesus. Second, he sees that God's righteousness triumphed in Jesus' death and resurrection and that as a result Jesus has been elevated to the "right hand of God" (Eph. 1:20) and designated as "Lord." Third, he sees that in Jesus the devil has been judged and thus all who follow "the prince of the power of the air" likewise stand liable to judgment. God will give the just reward to all human needs. "And of this he has given assurance to all men by raising him [Jesus] from the dead" (Acts 17:31).

Application
1/We understand from Scripture that the convincing work of the Holy Spirit is usually carried out in conjunction with the verbal witness of Christians (Jn. 15:26-27). What does this suggest for your verbal witness, regarding its necessity and its content?

2/When you confront opposition to Christian truth, how should you respond?

3/What in this study reminds you about ways in which you need to rely on the Holy Spirit's work?

Further Study

1/*I Believe in the Holy Spirit* (Eerdmans, 1973) by Michael Green is an excellent book on the Holy Spirit.

2/Consider the relation between the work of the Holy Spirit and human nature (as described in Eph. 2:1-10). How do they "fit" together in the design of God's truth?

Romans 10:1-17

Questions

1/What does Paul say about the way the Jews try to achieve their salvation? What is the proper way to become right with God?

_____

_____

_____

2/To be right with God, what is a person not to do? (Verses 6-10 are a commentary on Deut. 30:11-14; read those verses to aid understanding.)

_____

_____

3/Where is the word that is necessary for salvation? What word is "on your lips"? What word is "in your heart"?

_____

_____

_____

_____

4/What causes those words of faith to be where Paul says
they are? Why is the preaching of the gospel necessary for
someone to be saved?

_____

_____

_____

Comments
Paul stated in Ephesians 2:8 that a person is saved *by* grace,
through faith. Grace, in this context, is the work of God the
Holy Spirit, bringing new life to a person. Faith is the person's response to the work of God's grace.

The meaning of faith is explained here by a contrast.
The opposite of having faith is not doubting, but is endeav-
oring by some means to curry God's favor. But the salvation
of which Paul speaks is not obtained by scurrying about
looking everywhere to find a way to please God. Salvation
comes through resting in the confidence that God's grace
is already active in one's behalf. The Christian message says,
"Man, quit your fussing about, trying to obtain God's favor.
Relax. God loves you. He accepts you."

The proof of God's grace is found in Jesus Christ. God
raised him from the dead and made him Lord. The human
response in regeneration, then, comes when someone lets
these words fall from his lips: "Jesus is Lord." When someone does this, it is the Holy Spirit at work (1 Cor. 12:3). The

Holy Spirit puts the belief in the heart and the words in the mouth. A person can know he is saved if he finds himself believing that God accepts him and acknowledging that Jesus is Lord, for this can be done only by the work of the Holy Spirit.

Application

1/It is appropriate to remind yourself that you do not depend on anything in yourself to cause God to think well of you. The response of faith rests in God's grace alone. Praise God for his grace.

2/What responsibility do you have toward nonbelievers based on verse 17? How will you fulfill this?

Further Study

1/Read "Divine Sovereignty and Human Responsibility," chapter 2 in J. I. Packer's *Evangelism and the Sovereignty of God* (IVP, 1961).

2/Why is belief in the resurrection of Jesus essential to salvation? Paul says that Jesus was "raised for our justification" (Rom. 4:25); Peter says that "we have been born anew . . . through the resurrection of Jesus Christ" (1 Pet. 1:3). What is the significance of these statements?

study 5
the result

Galatians 5:16-25

Questions

1/What does Paul command his readers to do and not to do in vv. 16-17? What is the meaning of each? What reason does Paul give for obeying these commands?

_____

_____

_____

_____

2/Analyze carefully the list of the "works of the flesh." What kinds of actions are mentioned?

_____

_____

_____

3/What is the result for those who do the works of the flesh?

_____

_____

4/Analyze carefully the list of the "fruit of the Spirit." What kinds of actions are in view?

_____

_____

_____

5/The actions of verses 19-21 are called "works"; those of verses 22 and 23 are called "fruit." What is the significance of this difference?

_____

_____

Comments

The regenerating work of the Holy Spirit leads a person to the inward response of faith. It also leads to external change, which is sometimes called _conversion._ The root idea of the word _conversion_ is that of radical redirection of action. Before regeneration we naturally manifest the works of the flesh which come as a result of the condition of sin (compare Mk. 7:20-23). But after the Holy Spirit regenerates a person, a different manifestation begins to appear— the sublime virtues of Christian faith.

Conversion of this sort is to be expected from someone who is truly born of God. Absence of the fruit of the Spirit is reason to doubt a person's regeneration. Jesus himself gave us this principle (Mt. 7:16-18). Of course, one does not manifest all the fruit of the Spirit perfectly and immediately. The Christian experience is a development. As one matures, the fruit ripens.

Application

1/What "works of the flesh" are still sometimes present in your life? What will you do about it?

_____

_____

_____

2/How can you help the fruit of the Spirit ripen in your conduct today? Which varieties of the fruit does God seem to be cultivating most in you right now?

_____

_____

_____

_____

Further Study
1/*In Understanding Be Men*, pp. 152-159.
2/Michael Green, *New Life, New Lifestyle* (IVP, 1973).

topic d
REGENERATION BY THE SPIRIT

study 6
life of the spirit

Romans 8:1-17

Questions

1/What was the purpose of God's sending Jesus as a man, according to this section? What is the Christian's relationship to the law, then?

_____

_____

_____

2/Paul contrasts the flesh and the Spirit. List the elements of contrast.

_____

_____

_____

3/What assures a person that it is not necessary to live in continual sin?

_____

4/What promise for the future is given to one who has the Spirit?

5/How is one assured that he has been regenerated?

Comments

To be born again is to begin a new life. The idea of rebirth is very striking; nothing could picture a more profound change than this. But that is just what it is to change from living "in the flesh," to living "in the Spirit."

"In the flesh" a person can only sin. He does not obey God's law because it is impossible for him to do so. The only way we can meet God's requirements is for us to be given a whole new source of life. This was made possible by Jesus' life, death and resurrection. Now we who have been made righteous through his resurrection can obey God's law. To be sure, we are not regenerated by obeying God's law. But since God's law is holy and good, the Spirit who is himself "holy" will produce a lifestyle that fulfills God's moral requirements. Regenerate persons obey God's law not because of some external compulsion, but because that is the natural inclination produced by the work of the Holy Spirit.

How do we know that we have been reborn by the Spirit?

First we are inclined to obey God's law; and then we face a conflict that such an inclination produces (see Rom. 7: 15-25). Second, we discover on our lips and in our hearts an acknowledgment that Jesus is the living Lord. We discover in our lives a motivating force producing love and the Christian lifestyle. Third, we discover the inner inclination to call God "Father" because we have been reconciled to him.

Application
1/How do you "put to death the deeds of the body" today?

_____

_____

2/How are you fulfilling the "just requirement of the law" in your actions?

_____

_____

_____

3/What specific things are you reminded of in this study for which you will thank God?

_____

_____

Further Study
1/*Men Made New* (IVP, 1966) by John R. W. Stott is a lucid exposition of this section of Scripture and the preceding chapters.
2/John's first letter focuses on indications and assurances or tests of personal regeneration. Study it, compiling a list of the evidences by which you can tell that you are regenerate.

topic d
REGENERATION BY THE SPIRIT

summary

Write concise responses to the following:

1/This is what I believe about regeneration:

_____

_____

_____

_____

_____

2/This is the impact that belief has on my life:

_____

_____

_____

_____

3/These are my questions about the Holy Spirit's work of regeneration:

---

topic e
JESUS' RETURN

"The expectation
of the personal return
of our Lord Jesus Christ."

The New Testament declares in unmistakable language that Jesus Christ will return to the world at some time in the future. W. Griffith Thomas wrote: "The Lord's coming is referred to in one verse out of every thirteen in the New Testament, and in the Epistles alone in one verse out of ten. This proportion is surely of importance, for if frequency of mention is any criterion there is scarcely any other truth of equal interest and value." (Quoted in *Evangelical Belief,* Inter-Varsity Fellowship, 1961.)

Of the five topics in this guide, this one has produced the widest divergence among evangelicals themselves. Disagreements have divided them into distinct groupings with grandiose labels, such as premillennialists, postmillennialists, amillennialists, dispensationalists and so forth. The study of future things (eschatology) has sometimes engrossed evangelical believers in elaborate speculation and dogmatizing, much of which seems to be more like "Christianized" astrology than reverent Bible study. In reaction, many evangelicals have paid too little attention to this topic which figures so prominently in the Bible.

We must avoid the extremes of ignoring the Bible's teaching about Jesus' return, on the one hand, and of excessive fascination with the future so that we ignore the rest of the Bible's teaching, on the other. We are responsible to study what God has given to us in the Scripture.

The approach taken in this guide emphasizes what Jesus himself taught about his return. Within that teaching, the guide stresses what can be determined for certain and goes lightly over what appears to be open to dispute. Jesus left no doubt about what he wanted his followers to know for sure.

**topic e
JESUS' RETURN**

**study 1
jesus will return**

Acts 1:6-11; 1 Thessalonians 4:13—5:4

Questions

1/Acts 1:6-11. According to Jesus, what is the extent of his disciples' knowledge? What was the extent of his command to them?

_____

_____

_____

2/What did the two men in white promise to the disciples?

_____

_____

3/1 Thessalonians 4:13—5:4. What similarities do you find between Paul's statement to the Thessalonian believers and that of the two men in white?

_____

_____

4/What information does Paul add to that of the two men?

5/On what two settled facts of history is the belief in the future coming of Jesus Christ based? Why?

6/What does the reference to a thief illustrate about Jesus' return?

Comments
Jesus is coming back. The Jesus who was God in the flesh, who died, and who rose from death will return to this world for his followers. Jesus promised this himself (Jn. 14:3) and that promise was repeated by others.

Subsequent studies in this topic will uncover some details about the New Testament view of Jesus' return. This study opens the topic by laying out the straightforward fact: Jesus will return. When he will return is an open question; both passages point to this. But both insist that the events of the past stand as a guarantee that Jesus will return. Since Jesus rose from death, believers know for sure that they too will be resurrected to eternal life. When the disciples saw Jesus ascend into heaven they witnessed the first part of a two-part sequence. Just as Jesus ascended into heaven, he will return from heaven.

Application

1/Why can Christian believers have joy when others have sorrow? How do you experience this?

_____

_____

_____

2/Some things about God are pointed to in these sections. Identify them and worship him for them.

_____

_____

_____

Further Study

1/What implications can you identify in Paul's referring to Jesus' return as "the Day of the Lord"? (See Is. 2:11-13; 13:6-13; Ezek. 30:3; Joel 2:1-2, 11, 28-32; Amos 5:18-20; 1 Cor. 1:8.)

2/*In Understanding Be Men*, pp. 188-193.

3/Stephen Travis, *The Jesus Hope* (IVP, 1976).

study 2
jesus discusses his return

Matthew 24:1-31

Questions

1/To what is Jesus' declaration in verses 4-31 a response? What does their question show about the disciples' thinking?

_____

_____

_____

2/List the things Jesus says will happen subsequent to the time of his speaking. State, where possible, what he says these events will indicate.

_____

_____

_____

_____

_____

3/Compose a brief summary characterizing the events.

4/What does Jesus' use of the simile of lightning show about his return?

Comments
The disciples showed their normal human curiosity to know about the future when they asked Jesus to explain his prediction. But they also showed their confusion when they asked what really amounted to two different questions: When will Jerusalem be destroyed? and When will Jesus return? They did not realize, as we now do, that these events were to be separated by at least 1900 years. Jesus'

response, then, entails two answers, partly entangled with each other. Bible students have disagreed over the way in which they are to be disentangled. Some verses apparently refer to the destruction of Jerusalem; some to the end of history, when Jesus will return; and some may even refer to both events.

When teaching in Scripture confuses us, it is best to start by culling out what can be established as certain. Here three points, at least, are clear. First, Jesus stated that he would return to gather his followers to himself. Second, there would be severe hardship in the years between his first and second comings. Third, Jesus' return will be no secret when it occurs. It will be a public event, not a hidden one.

Application
1/How does Jesus' teaching instruct you to respond to reports of wars, earthquakes, false religious teaching and widespread immorality?

_____

_____

_____

2/How does Jesus' statement in verse 14 affect your interest in worldwide Christian missionary activity?

_____

_____

Further Study
1/What implications can you draw from the warning with which Jesus begins his teaching? We have observed that in Matthew's recording of this teaching there is a complex interweaving of references to two future events, one close to Jesus' time

and the other obviously in the distant future. What implications can you draw from this structure?

2/Study 2 Thessalonians 2:1-12 and compare it to Matthew 24:24-27.

**study 3
when will he come?**

Matthew 24:32-51

Questions

1/List each declaration that Jesus makes about the time of his return.

_____

_____

_____

_____

_____

2/In verses 36-44, four illustrations are given. What one point are they all making?

_____

_____

_____

3/In 45-51, what is the heart of the servant's mistake?

4/What point does Jesus make with the illustration about the servant?

Comments

It is a certain fact that Jesus will return. It is the most certain fact of the future, for Jesus said he would return and then gave the solemn declaration that though "heaven and earth will pass away, my words will not pass away." But just as the *fact* of Jesus' return is unshakable, the *time* of his return is unknown and unknowable to us.

The disciples specifically asked Jesus to tell them when he would return. Jesus' words are, in part, a response to that request to know the time when he will come. But they are not an answer to the disciples' question. Jesus speaks evasively, in negative terms. He even says he does not know the answer, nor does that seem to concern him. Instead he shows that he considers something to be much more important than knowledge about the date. That is readiness for the event.

Jesus' return will be sudden and there is therefore the danger that it will catch his followers by surprise. Jesus views such a surprise as a tragic prospect. And so he hammers home his point. His followers must be prepared for his return at *any* time. Mark reports that Jesus added at this point, "What I say to you I say to all: Watch: (Mk. 13:37). The person who is looking for Jesus' return shows that he is a true follower of the Lord; the person who calls himself Christian but is unprepared is a hypocrite and will receive his just reward.

The true Christian is the one who lives in readiness for Jesus' return, not the one who speculates about when it might happen.

Application

1/To what extent do you actively anticipate Jesus' return?

_____

_____

2/How can you be prepared for Jesus' return? Analyze the illustration of the servant and think of specific applications for your life. What was he supposed to be doing? What was he doing?

_____

_____

_____

Further Study

1/This section contains one of the most troublesome predictions of all Scripture—verse 34. Did Jesus say that he would return before some people then living had died? If he did, our confidence in all he said must be shaken. Christians know that these words must mean something different. To what does "generation" refer? Contemporaries of Jesus? a race of people? contemporaries of "these things"? To what does "these things" refer? Jesus' return? fall of Jerusalem? the whole plan of God for history? Christians have adopted various combinations of these as an explanation. I am inclined toward the understanding that Jesus predicted Jerusalem would be destroyed within the lifetime of some of his disciples.

2/Speculations about the time of the end of the world and of Jesus' return have recently become especially common, not only among Christians but also among adherents of other views. What should be the attitude of Christians toward the speculations of those who pay attention to indicators additional to God's Word? (See Deut. 18:9-12, 21-22; Is. 8:19-20; Jer. 10:2; Ezek. 13:1-7; 2 Tim. 2:14-18.)

**study 4
ready for his coming**

Matthew 25:1-30

Questions

1/In the first story, what is the chief difference between the wise and foolish women?

_____

_____

2/What is the primary point that Jesus makes with this story?

_____

_____

3/What is the function of the "for" that begins the second story?

_____

_____

_____

4/Diagram the story in the following chart:

	Given	Action	Reward
First servant	_____	_____	_____
Second servant	_____	_____	_____
Third servant	_____	_____	_____

5/What are the differences among the servants?

_____

_____

_____

_____

6/State the point Jesus makes with this story.

_____

_____

Comments

In these parables Jesus elaborates his chief concern regarding his return: the readiness of his followers. It is possible that the stories Jesus uses relate events that actually occurred. They reflect common practices of Jesus' time. Jesus sees in them the vivid lesson that human beings can easily be lazy, irresponsible and unprepared.

With the story of the virgins, Jesus suggests that his return might not occur as soon as people expect it. His main point is that even if the expected arrival seems to be delayed, the wise follower will keep himself prepared. With the story of the three servants, Jesus illustrates his understanding of preparedness. It entails more than thinking and talking about Jesus' return. God has given certain responsibilities to each Christian. One's responsibility may be in the form of a position, office or job; another's may be education, training or opportunity; another's may be money; another's may be gifts and abilities. Faithfulness in fulfilling these responsibilities constitutes the preparation to which Jesus calls his followers.

Application

1/What warnings do you hear in this section?

_____

_____

2/Examine yourself. What "talents" has God given you? How are you exercising your responsibilities faithfully?

_____

_____

3/To what evidence can you point to show that you are prepared for Jesus' return?

_____

_____

Further Study

1/Examine how Mark's report of this sermon (Mk. 13:33-37) includes a composite of the points of Matthew 24:45-51 and 25:14-30.
2/Notice what Luke 19:11-27 indicates is the purpose of the second parable.
3/What parallels in word choice can you find in comparing the first story here with Matthew 7:24-27? What do these imply?

study 5
the judgment

Matthew 25:31-46

Questions

1/When are the events Jesus describes to occur?

2/Who will be gathered before the Son of man?

3/To whom does Jesus refer as the "King"? What is the significance of this?

4/On what basis does the King assign eternal punishment or eternal life to those who stand before him? What claim about himself is Jesus making?

_____

_____

_____

5/Write a concise statement of the essential difference between the "sheep" and the "goats."

_____

_____

_____

_____

6/What does Jesus teach about life and time after his return?

_____

_____

_____

Comments

From the lips of Jesus himself we receive the most complete description in all of Scripture of the determination of the final destiny of all people. After death there will be a judgment; we all will appear before the court of Jesus Christ to have our actions judged. That is what the rest of the New Testament also declares (2 Cor. 5:10; Heb. 9:27; 1 Cor. 3:10-15; Rom. 14:10-12; Rev. 20:11-15). In Matthew 25:31-46 Jesus informs us of the true basis of the final discrimination among people.

The crucial distinction among people, Jesus indicates, is the way they relate to him; and the way we treat people around us is the way we relate to Jesus. Jesus points specifically to actions which meet people's human needs. Jesus does not suggest that a person can earn a way into heaven by doing acts of charity. He simply underscores the truth that only charitable people have the love of God in them (1 Jn. 3:16-18), and that whoever shows love in action has been born again by the Holy Spirit (1 Jn. 4:7).

Application
1/How does your life show evidence that you are one of Jesus' sheep?

2/How can you meet the physical and psychological needs of other people today? Think through the application of this truth toward: lonely people, people with financial difficulties, a student having academic problems, needy people in your town, victims of oppression.

Further Study

1/*In Understanding Be Men,* pp. 193-202.

2/Compare this description (Mt. 25:31-46) with that in Matthew 7:15-23. What important differences do you find?

3/Some Christians have tried to avoid the punch of this study by a twisted interpretation of Jesus' words which removes their relevance to us today. Claiming that Jesus' description teaches a "salvation by works," these interpreters say, for example, that Jesus is not speaking about the judgment of all individuals who have ever lived, or they assert that he is speaking about "spiritual hunger and loneliness" rather than real, physical hunger. How can these ideas be refuted? Some focus on the word "nations" and insist that this is a judgment of countries, not individuals. What evidence in the text refutes this idea? "Nations" is the New Testament word for "people of the world" (cf. Mt. 28:19). To whom does "brethren" refer? (See Mt. 12:46-50; 28:10; Heb. 2:11; 1 Jn. 3:10, 14-18; Gal. 6:10; Rom. 13:8; Lk. 10:29-37.)

4/Reflect on the word Jesus uses to describe those who receive eternal life (Mt. 25:37, 46). What implications can you find in the designation "righteous" for the "sheep"? Compare the following verses where the same Greek word is used to describe people: Matthew 1:19; 10:41; 13:49; Acts 10:22; Romans 1:17; 2:13. What does it mean to be "just"? What is the relationship between the quality of being "just" or "righteous" and the actions which Jesus ascribes to the "sheep"?

**topic e
JESUS' RETURN**

**study 6
living for jesus' return**

1 Peter 4:7-11; Titus 2:11-14; Hebrews 10:23-25

Questions

1/List all the things that believers are told to *do* in these passages.

_____

_____

_____

_____

_____

2/What ideas are common to each of these three writers as they consider the Lord's return?

_____

_____

_____

3/What does the Lord's return entail for the believer's relationship with other Christians? Relate this to the servant in study 3.

_____

_____

_____

_____

Comments

The fact that Jesus Christ is coming again is not to be a matter for idle, impractical contemplation and speculation. Our interest in this future event must not cause us to escape from the present situations of our lives. The New Testament writers did not know when Jesus would return. But they obeyed his words and lived as if he would return soon. The fact that he will return led them to live and advocate a particular way of life. Because Jesus will return, they said, you must be more active in your expression of love to fellow Christians. God has entrusted you with certain "talents" that he expects you to exercise responsibly while you have the opportunity.

Hebrews 10:23-25 points out a corollary to this. Christians should encourage and help each other to find ways to fulfill their responsibilities. The Christian lifestyle is a community lifestyle.

Application

1/Refer to your list in question 1. Think through how you can follow these specifically in your life.

_____

_____

_____

_____

_____

2/Is there an action in your life you must change or perform more diligently?

_____

_____

3/Would you feel prepared if Jesus were to return today? Why?

_____

_____

_____

_____

Further Study

1/There are many other references in the New Testament to Jesus' return, similar to those studied here. As you read the New Testament, make a list of all such references. Notice how the idea that Jesus would return penetrated the thinking of the early Christians, and what application they made of it.

2/Most Christians are aware that the last book of the New Testament says a lot about Jesus' return; but most Christians are confused by this book. One helpful, nontechnical discussion of the Revelation is _I Saw Heaven Opened_ (IVP, 1975), by Michael Wilcock.

3/Read _The Meaning of the Millennium_ (IVP, 1977) edited by Robert Clouse for a discussion of the four dominant views of the millennium.

topic e
JESUS' RETURN

summary

Write concise responses to the following:

1/This is what I believe about Jesus' return:

_____

_____

_____

_____

2/This is the impact that belief has on my life:

_____

_____

_____

_____

3/These are my questions about Jesus' return:

_____

_____

_____

_____

_____

for further study from InterVarsity Press

GETTING TO KNOW GOD
In this companion volume to *Getting to Know Your Faith*, Paul Steeves presents thirty Bible studies which take up the doctrine of God: his nature, sovereignty, holiness, goodness and love. paper, $1.75

GETTING TO KNOW JESUS
Paul Steeves supplies daily studies in the same format as the present volume, exploring what Scripture tells us about Jesus' deity, lordship, love, death and resurrection. paper, $1.75

IN UNDERSTANDING BE MEN
T. C. Hammond outlines the major Christian doctrines, presents divergent views and their bases, then lists relevant Scripture passages. A good follow-up to *Getting to Know Your Faith*. paper, $3.95

DECIDE FOR YOURSELF: A THEOLOGICAL WORKBOOK
Gordon R. Lewis helps you to think through Christian doctrines in the context of many alternatives and to work out your own conclusions. It will be helpful if you can discuss your findings in a group. paper, $2.50

JUDGE FOR YOURSELF: A WORKBOOK ON CONTEMPORARY CHALLENGES TO CHRISTIAN FAITH
Gordon R. Lewis takes up seven basic questions non-Christians ask, lists the possible answers and marshals the biblical evidence to help each reader come to his own conclusions. Companion to *Decide for Yourself*. paper, $2.95